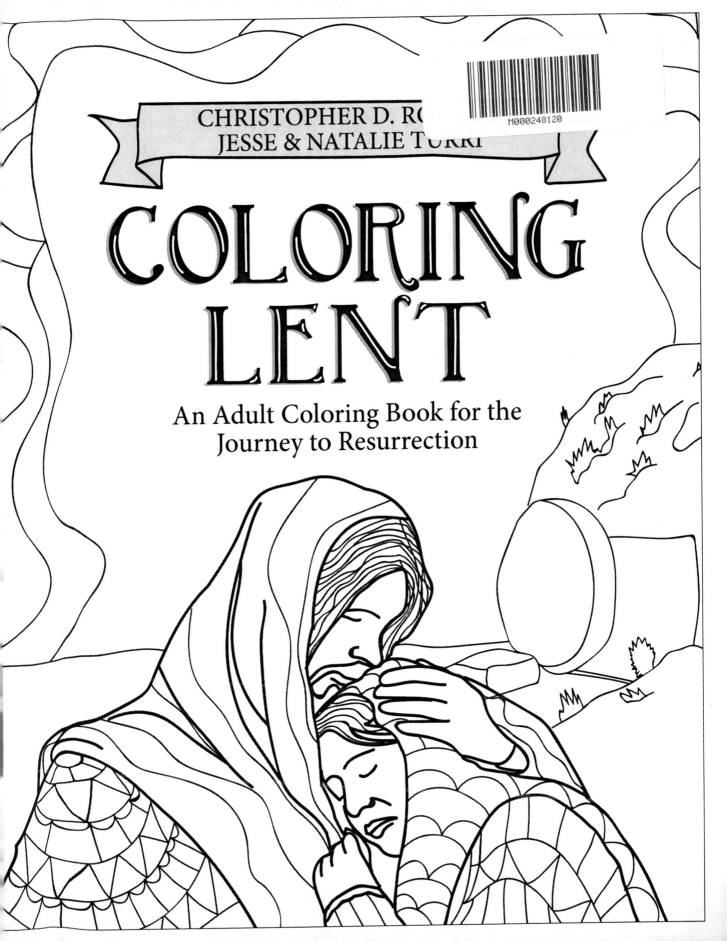

CHRISTOPHER D. RO
JESSE & NATALIE TURRI

COLORING
LENT

An Adult Coloring Book for the
Journey to Resurrection

Illustrations are by Natalie and Jesse Turri.
Text is by Christopher Rodkey. Text in quotes, unless otherwise cited, is the author's paraphrase of scripture.

CBPBooks.com

ISBN: 9780827205475

COLORING LENT

CONTENTS

THE RESURRECTION OF THE BODY: A THEOLOGICAL INTRODUCTION

Christians throughout the world prepare for Lent by observing Transfiguration Sunday, which is the final Sunday of the Epiphany, and Clean Monday, celebrated by Eastern Christians as a day of the purging of sin, and flying kites. Some then have a feast on Shrove Tuesday; in my Pennsylvania Dutch heritage we call it "Fastnacht Day"; other parts of the world call it Mardi Gras, Terça-feira Gorda (Fat Tuesday), or Vielchendienstag (Violet Tuesday).

Lent formally begins on Ash Wednesday and ends on Holy Saturday. Thematically Lent is the journey from the death of the body to the death of God—a death that is then reversed in hell so that in this world, the remains of an anointed corpse begin breathing newly. This moment of Easter is Good News for this Jesus, who is fully human and fully God, yet it is even better news for the world: God has not only moved into the world with humans but the fullness of God has taken on flesh. And Easter, we should remember, is only a provisional period before the Ascension of Christ disseminates the Holy Spirit upon all flesh on the Day of Pentecost. Easter is a season, and Easter is a lifestyle, but we should not lose sight of the fact that this mystery and miracle of Easter is only a short time in the scheme of history, and the greatest acts of God have yet to come though the enfleshment of God's people—us.

As you color these pages, then, consider how your fingertips, your palms, your body have now become the habitat of God, and following the stories of the Hebrew and New Testaments, consider how we might also walk the same journey of Jesus.

Like Jesus' path, ours calls us to transfiguration. Each step of our walk is part of an eschatological vision. We can make this moment dazzling and spectacular through self-giving acts and by transforming those places where we only find death to become brimming with life. As James Cone teaches, the same "eschatological vision" of Jesus' transfiguration is sparked in everyday people, whether it was St. Paul on the road to Damascus; Malcolm X in prison; or Martin Luther King, Jr., listening to God's call to justice in his kitchen. Our call to transfiguration comes in what would seem to be the most banal of moments. The liberation of those who are named as blessed in the Beatitudes arrives through transfigured moments of people of every race, class, gender, and nationality.[1]
The journey of Christ leads us all as individuals on this journey in the hope of a true Mass of transfiguration as a church.

Jesus proclaimed a total transformation of society: the entire social order must be transfigured for the sake of the Kingdom of God—that is, the last of this world. Jesus did more than preach about a radical reversal of the world, but, as Thomas Altizer observes, Jesus "enacted a total transformation of everything," that is, "a transformation which is the advent of the kingdom of God."[2] In the New Creation that is Now Occurring[3] in us and through us when we live the cruciform life, with our hands and with our feet we work for the Kingdom. The Kingdom may be in a state of a perpetual "not-yet," but our ministry must be within this liminal space between "not-yet" and the Kingdom.

Catherine Keller reminds us in her theopoetic and mystical book *Cloud of the Impossible* of the long tradition of the image or metaphor of "the cloud," which is employed throughout this present work. The "cloud" is referenced even through the borders of the pages in this book. Clouds are phenomena, Keller writes, of the primal elements, "of Shifting Intensities of the Sun's heat interactively producing earth's vapors from its waters."[4] A genuine Lenten discipline is not only an inward journey, but one that leads us to recognize that our spirit is not what is prioritized in a resurrection, but rather—as the historic creeds affirm—our bodies are resurrected; from the heat of the Sun, we shall be stirred vaporously and viscerally to serve and prioritize the suffering of this material world, this bodily plane.

Our Lenten discipline must lead us to live cruciform-shaped lives in self-giving and bold ways, recognizing that, as Jesus whispered to Nicodemus in secret, God loved this world so much that God's son was given for it, we are emboldened when the dispensation of scripture has been seemingly silenced. But even further, as a church, when we embody and enflesh the still-speaking God, we affirm that this same God who pours out Godself into a Son and pours out Spirit into all flesh on the Day of Pentecost, to invoke the words of Gabriel Vahanian, "entrusts the world with God."[5] That which was once regal has been relegated and invested into our hands and feet. May we color our worlds with this exquisite responsibility as renewed, restored resurrection people.

Christopher D. Rodkey

Notes

1. James Cone, *The Cross and the Lynching Tree* (Maryknoll, NY: Orbis, 2011), 155.

2. Thomas J. J. Altizer, *The Contemporary Jesus* (Albany, NY: SUNY P, 1997), 6.

3. This is a term I employ in my theology of preaching, taken after the theological language of D. G. Leahy; Christopher Rodkey, *Too Good to Be True* (Winchester, UK: Christian Alternative, 2014), 17-19.

4. Catherine Keller, *Cloud of the Impossible* (New York: Columbia UP, 2014), 313-314.

5. Gabriel Vahanian, *Theopoetics of the Word* (New York: Palgrave Macmillan, 2014), 52.

Baptized

A PREFACE: THE CLOUD TRANSFIGURES

Jesus came to John the Baptist and asked to be baptized in the Jordan River.

As Jesus arose from the baptismal waters, the Cloud transfigured, irrevocably and annularly tore apart, and descended the Holy Spirit upon Jesus like a dove.

The Cloud speaks out of exhaustion: "This is my Son."

So begins the final descent of the Cloud into human death; the Cloud now being nailed onto the cross of humanity.

Matthew 3, Mark 1, Luke 3, John 1

To Drink From Your Fountain...

EPIGRAPH: A PRAYER FOR CLEAN MONDAY

Your Word is a Tree of Life offering us blessed fruit from each of its branches. Your Word is like that rock which was struck open in the wilderness, from which all are offered spiritual drink.

Let us be thankful for the overabundant gifts given to us, and not be saddened that the overabundance discloses our human limitations. Because the Fountain of Your Word is inexhaustible, let our thirst for You be satisfied without believing that Your Fountain is exhaustible.

As we are again thirsty, we return to Your Word to drink from Your fountain. Lend us Your illumination that we might not be arrested before the awe of how much more we might absorb when we return again and again.

Amen.

After St. Ephrem the Syrian†

Led Away

LENT DAY 1: ASH WEDNESDAY

This is a journey of clouded darkness, a journey of gloom and thick darkness! Just as Jesus and the disciples were surrounded by the Cloud, and the Israelites followed the Cloud through the wilderness, be mindful of the Cloud that surrounds you, and do not take it for granted!

May we live the cruciform life in this season of Lent, mindful of the absolute exhaustion of God into Christ. May we be led away from the false gods of money, government, and hierarchical religion to a life aspiring toward perfection.

For the little bird that believes itself to be free seemingly strikes the walls of its cage! Seek liberation by going deeper. Practice liberation by following the Cloud to the larger work of healing the world. Amen.

Joel 2, Philippians 2†

The Serpent Tempts

LENT DAY 2:

AROUND THE BEGINNING

The serpent tempts Adam and Eve in the Garden of Eden, enacting the fall of humanity. Human sinfulness enters the world for the very first time, and with it, death and labor.

Genesis 3, Romans 5

Violence is Their Answer

LENT DAY 3: CHILDREN OF ADAM

In a rage of jealousy over the favor of God, Cain kills his brother Abel, the first act of fracturing human community, enacting violence into the world.

The Cloud shrieks: "Cain, what have you done? Your brother's blood cries out from the stones and dirt of the earth!"

Cain's descendants are the "Children of Wrath": Violence is their answer for every human problem.

Genesis 4, Ephesians 2†

God Makes a Covenant

LENT DAY 4: AFTER THE FLOOD

God makes a covenant with Noah, his children, and all flesh—all of the animals—that whenever the Cloud covers the earth and the rainbow is displayed, this promise shall be remembered: God will always honor the covenant to never again use violence to solve the problems of humans, angels, or Nephilim.

Genesis 9

Will We Too Live Again?

LENT DAY 5 (FIRST SUNDAY OF LENT): JOB MEDITATES ON DEATH AND NEW LIFE

Job asks the meaning of human life in light of the reality of human death, saying, "Even if a tree is cut down, out of its stump will shoot sprouts and new life springing out of what appears to be death."

Job prays in hope: "Hide me in the darkness of death, and remember me! Will we too live again?"

Job 14†

Priest of the Cloud

LENT DAY 6: THE ORDER OF MELCHIZEDEK

Returning home from battle, Abram meets with the King of Sodom. Abram had kept his previous promises to God.

Melchizedek, the King of Salem and Priest of the Cloud, blesses Abram and gives him bread and wine to nourish his army. Abram in return gives a tenth of all spoils of war to Melchizedek. Melchizedek is both a king and high priest; much later Jesus would continue and extend his order of priesthood to all.

Genesis 14, Hebrews 5

The Darkness of the Cloud

LENT DAY 7: THE PROMISE TO ABRAM

The Word of God comes to Abram in a vision and blesses him further, predicting that his descendants will be more than the stars of the sky.

Amazed and perplexed, Abram offers an animal sacrifice to God. Falling into a deep sleep at sundown, the darkness of the Cloud covers him. He awakes to see a smoking fire pot and a torch of flame passing between the parts of the sacrifice!

The Cloud does this according to ancient ritual custom, indicating that this promise is completely unconditional.

Genesis 15

Promise Would Be Kept

LENT DAY 8: HOPING AGAINST HOPE

The Cloud made a promise to Abram when he was much younger that he would be made into a great nation. Hoping against hope, by the age of 99, Abram remains faithful in believing that this promise would be kept. The Cloud proclaims again that Abram's descendants will be numerous and this promise will remain throughout the generations.

With the Cloud renaming him "Abraham," the everlasting covenant is established with those who are not only his blood descendants but also his spiritual heirs, which is the entire world.

Genesis 17, Romans 4

Passover

LENT DAY 9: THE INSTITUTION OF THE PASSOVER

While the Israelites are in slavery in Egypt, the Cloud instructs that there be a ritual sacrifice of a lamb in every household; the blood of the lamb shall be placed on the exterior of their homes. While the Cloud passes over the city, dispensing judgment upon the oppressors, the unjust, and the gods who answer to humans, it will simply drift over the blood-marked homes.

The promises and instructions for preparation and eating together on this night are to be a new holiday, a festival remembering the Cloud "passing over."

Exodus 12

Water Flows

LENT DAY 10: WATER GUSHING FROM STONE

Wandering through the desert, the Israelites become desperately thirsty, and complain to Moses, "Why are we trusting in this God who has brought us all the way out to this desert of nothingness to die of thirst?"

The Cloud replies: "Go to the Rock of Horeb. There I will remain in front of you. Strike your staff upon the rock."

Moses does as commanded, and with the elders witnesses water flowing from the rock.

Exodus 17

Snakes Attack

LENT DAY 11:
SNAKES ON A PLAIN

The Israelites promise God that they will violently destroy their enemies if they have victory in battle. After the victory, the people again wander through the desert and complain loudly, blaming God for not providing food and water.

A plague of poisonous snakes attack the people, and many of them die. The Cloud instructs Moses to craft the Nehushtan, a bronze serpent hung on a pole after the ancient serpent cult traditions. All who look upon it will be healed of their snakebite wounds.

Numbers 21†

The Cloud Rains Down

LENT DAY 12 (SECOND SUNDAY OF LENT):
THEOPHANY AT MT. SINAI

Moses climbs to the top of Mount Sinai and the Cloud rains down the Ten Commandments. This new foundation of human law is rooted in the rejection of idolatry, since all sin from the time of Adam and Cain is rooted in self-idolatry and leads to false beliefs in a God of Violence.

Hearing this, the Israelites are afraid that the words from the Cloud will cause them to die. Moses responds, "The Cloud does not wish you to sin and cause violence to each other."

Exodus 19—20

The Serpent Under Your Feet

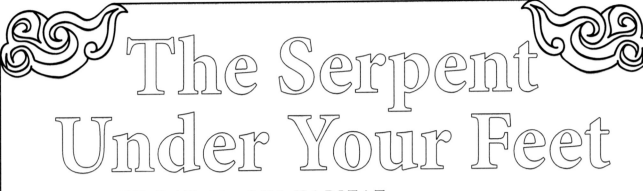

LENT DAY 13: QUI HABITAT

Although no one knows for certain who wrote the beautiful words of Psalm 91, many believe that it was written by Moses, singing before his death:

"God's angels will be commanded to guard you in all of your ways, and they will raise you up, so that your feet will never dash a stone, you will stomp down the lion and the serpent under your feet!"

Psalm 91†

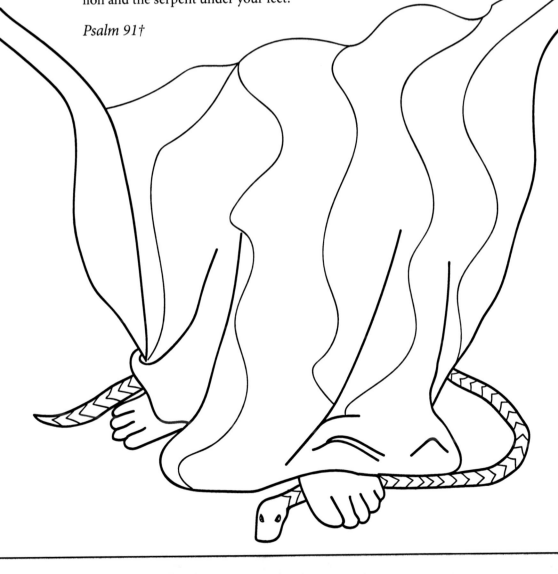

God's Laws Re-established

LENT DAY 14: THE SECOND PASSOVER

After Moses dies, Joshua, when finally arriving at Gilgal on the plains of Jericho, orders that God's laws be re-established and practiced according to the instructions given to Moses in the "spoken law" of the Torah. The manna that the Cloud had offered the people ceases. They can now survive off the land and can grow crops.

The Passover is celebrated for the first time outside of Egypt in the promised land.

Joshua 5

The Weeping Prophet

LENT DAY 15: A NEW KIND OF COVENANT

Before the Exile, the weeping prophet Jeremiah proclaims that the Cloud will never give up on God's people, and that a new kind of covenant is coming. The people will know and be taught by God directly, and their former and recent sins will be absolved.

Jeremiah 31

God Lives Here

LENT DAY 16: EZEKIEL'S FINAL VISION

During the Exile, and toward the end of his life, the priest Ezekiel prophesies of a future Final Temple, when the Cloud will descend to dwell among the people in an ultimate Holy City.

In the vision, the Cloud carries Ezekiel to the top of the highest mountain to view this future. He sees a man whose appearance is bronze—like the serpent set on Moses' staff—dressed as a priest entering the Temple and bearing a measuring rod in his hand! And the name of this place shall be "God lives there."

Ezekiel 40, 48

The Cloud Will Enter the World

LENT DAY 17: THE CLOUD WILL BE ENFLESHED

God speaks through an anonymous prophet: The Cloud will enter the diseased flesh of the world, and be wounded for our transgressions—and by his wounds we will be healed.

He will be like the sacrificial animal led to the slaughter to untangle the human logic of violence.

The Cloud will negate Itself by pouring out into flesh and into death.

Isaiah 52, 53†

This Is My Son!

INTERLUDE: THE TRANSFIGURATION OF JESUS

As Jesus and his disciples climb, the darkness of the Cloud surrounds and enshrouds the mountain. Suddenly Moses and Elijah appear, and as they speak with Jesus, his flesh is transfigured; he becomes dazzling white!

The Cloud announces again: "This is my son!" Then Elijah and Moses vanish; the Cloud dissipates.

Descending from the mountain, Jesus orders the disciples not to tell anyone what happened until the Kingdom is truly at hand, and all flesh is prepared for transfiguration.

Matthew 17, Mark 9, Luke 9

The Wilderness

LENT DAY 18: NOT BY BREAD ALONE

Filled with the Cloud, Jesus retreats into the desert wilderness, fasting for forty days and forty nights.

Satan tempts him while he is hungry, calling upon Jesus to transfigure the rocks on the ground into bread, like the manna provided for the Israelites in the desert. The wild beasts comfort Jesus, and the angels keep their distance, watching.

Matthew 4, Mark 1, Luke 4

Tempted

LENT DAY 19 (THIRD SUNDAY OF LENT): NOT TO BE TESTED

Taken to the highest peak of the Temple, Jesus is tempted by Satan to throw himself off the peak and into the graves of the ancients and call upon the angels to rescue him. Satan even quotes scripture by memory, singing the psalm of Moses.

Jesus looks directly down onto the tomb of Zechariah ben Jehoiada, the high priest who was killed in the court of the Temple by a mob, led by the King Joash, for preaching that the people had to repent and remember the laws given by the Cloud.

Jesus simply replies, "The Cloud is not to be tested."

2 Chronicles 24, Matthew 4, Luke 4†

The New Age is Dawning

LENT DAY 20:

THE BLIND NOW SEE

Jesus encounters a blind man. Jesus spits on the ground and spreads the mud made of his saliva and the dust of the ground onto the man's eyelids, and instructs him to wash in the Pool of Siloam.

This fulfills the prophecy spoken by the Cloud through Second Isaiah: "I proclaim this before it springs forth! I have offered a new covenant, a light to the nations that will open the eyes of the blind, release the prisoners from the dungeon, from the prison of Hell itself. Look! The former things of this world have passed away, and the New Age is dawning!"

Isaiah 42, John 9

He Weeps

LENT DAY 21: COME OUT!

Mary and Martha have sent a message to Jesus that their brother, Lazarus, whom Jesus loves, is ill and dying. Jesus goes to them, but Lazarus dies in the meantime. When Jesus arrives, he weeps, and asks to be taken to Lazarus's tomb.

A crowd of mourners—genuine and professional—are around the tomb, and Jesus orders the stone to be rolled away. The smell is overbearing, and Jesus approaches the entrance, calling upon the Cloud to draw near and listen.

"Come out!" Jesus commands. Lazarus emerges from the tomb.

Jesus thus steals the corpse of the social order, and many begin a plot to kill him.

John 11†

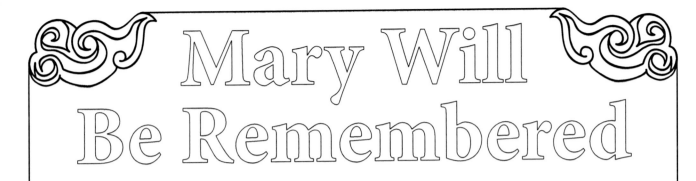

Mary Will Be Remembered

LENT DAY 22: IN BETHANY

Jesus and Judas visit Lazarus at his home, where Mary and Martha threw a dinner in Jesus' honor. Mary breaks open an alabaster jar containing pure spikenard, and wipes Jesus' feet with her hair as the fragrance fills the home.

Judas objects to this waste of the expensive oil, which was used to prepare bodies for burial and for ritual use. In the Temple, spikenard was part of the ceremonial incense offering of the "Ketoret," which represented substituted flesh sacrifices, burned daily before the thick curtain in the Sanctum Sanctorum.

Accepting Mary's hospitality, Jesus replies, "Wherever the Good News is preached throughout the world, Mary will be remembered for this important act of preserving my body."

Mark 14, John 12†

Shout Out!

LENT DAY 23: THE PARADE OF PALMS

To have the religious freedom to celebrate the Passover, the priests agree to allow the Emperor a Parade of Palms as a symbol of colonial triumph. The people come to the streets to patronizingly pay homage to Caesar Tiberius, "Son of the Divine."

Jesus asks his disciples to find a donkey for him to round out the parade as a parody and protest; the cityfolk lay down their coats and palm-branches to participate in the parody or to welcome Jesus as their savior into the Holy City.

The Pharisees order Jesus to silence his followers. "If they would be silent," he replies, "these stones of this Holy City would shout out the same blasphemy!"

Matthew 21, Mark 11, Luke 19, John 12†

And Not One Will Remain

LENT DAY 24: JERUSALEM! JERUSALEM!

Returning to the Mount of Olives, Jesus weeps in lament over the Holy City. "Jerusalem! Jerusalem!" he cries. "Like a mother hen, the Cloud has called you to unite the world under Her wings, and you refuse to listen!

"Only you can stone your own prophets! But the time is coming when the stones of the city walls will be surrounded, and not one will remain, and the Cloud will no longer surround the city."

Luke 13, 19

Drove Out

LENT DAY 25: THIS HOUSE IS NOT FOR SALE!

Again entering the city, Jesus comes near the Temple, and there sees the money changers who profit off of the priests' refusal to allow an image of the Empire on coins to enter the Temple—after allowing the Emperor to be worshiped in the streets out of political obligation.

Jesus makes a whip, overturns the money changers' tables, and drives the people and the animals out from the entrance to the Temple. He says, "As history has unfolded for our people, I will destroy this temple, and then raise up its body!"

Luke 19, John 2

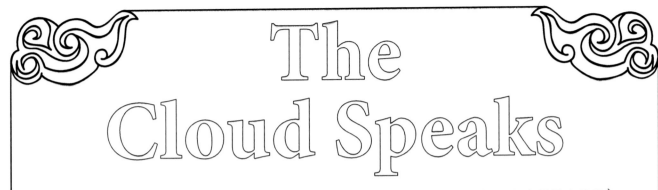

The Cloud Speaks

LENT DAY 26 (FOURTH SUNDAY OF LENT - LAETARE): I WILL BE RAISED

Some Greeks ask the disciple Philip whether Jesus could teach them. The Cloud breaks its silence to speak with thunder; some of the gathered crowd see an angel, and Jesus then turns to those assembled.

"The voice of the Cloud has spoken for you, but not for me," Jesus says. "Satan, who rules your world, is about to be expelled from the world.

"As for me, I will be lifted up from this earth, and draw everyone to me, and heal the nations. While the light shines upon you, let it shine while it remains with you. I did not enter this world to judge you, but to save you, to heal you from the darkness of the death of the body."

John 12

Not All Of You Are Clean

LENT DAY 27: NOT ALL OF YOU ARE CLEAN

Jesus hurriedly gathers his disciples for a Passover meal. Once they all arrive, Jesus takes off his robe, ties a towel around himself, and washes the disciples' feet. He says to Peter, "You are clean," turning to the disciples, "but not all of you are clean."

He then puts on his robe and teaches them. "If you are my disciples, and I your teacher, you should follow my example and wash one another's feet. Humble yourselves to each other, and love each other, as I have loved you."

John 13

Jesus Broke the Bread

LENT DAY 28: A REVERSAL OF PASSOVER

Jesus begins the Passover meal, but there is no lamb. What he has, Jesus offers to his disciples in the opposite order of tradition. First Jesus breaks the bread, blesses it, and says, "Eat, for this is my body."

Second, he takes the wine, instructing, "Drink, this is the Blood of the Covenant, poured out to atone for the sins of many."

Then Jesus teaches them. "I have looked forward to this Passover meal with all of you, but the sacrificial animal to be eaten will not be feasted upon until the Kingdom arrives."

Jesus then tells his followers that some will betray him. They all reply, "Not I, Rabbi?"

Jesus looks at Peter and prophesies, "You will not deny me once, but before the rooster crows in the morning, you will deny me three times!"

Matthew 26,
Mark 14,
Luke 22,
John 13

Jesus Collapses

LENT DAY 29: I AM DEEPLY GRIEVED

Leaving the Holy City and crossing out of the Kidron Valley, Jesus arrives at the Garden of Gethsemane, one of his favorite places to pray. Upon arrival, Jesus asks the disciples to keep watch while he prays.

In private, Jesus collapses onto the earth, sweating blood, and praying to the Cloud, "Abba, let this cup pass from me."

Meanwhile, the disciples fall asleep.

Matthew 26, Mark 14, Luke 22, John 18

Then They Arrest Him

LENT DAY 30: THE HOUR IS AT HAND

Judas arrives with the authorities to arrest Jesus and finds the disciples, sleeping.

Judas points at Jesus, saying, "This is my Teacher!" And Judas kisses Jesus; then they arrest him.

Matthew 26, Mark 14, Luke 22, John 18

Peter Draws A Sword

LENT DAY 31: PUT AWAY YOUR WEAPONS

Peter draws a sword and cuts off the ear of Malchus, a slave belonging to the High Priest.

Jesus admonishes his followers directly, "If you live by violence, you will die by violence!" Looking at the weapons of everyone gathered, Jesus teaches them with questions: "Do you not believe I can do what Satan has tempted me? Have I not spoken peacefully and faithfully in the Temple, and you never bothered to arrest me there?"

Before he is arrested, Jesus turns to the High Priest's slave and touches him, saying, "You have suffered enough." Malchus is healed.

Matthew 26, Mark 14,
Luke 22, John 18

They Are Afraid

LENT DAY 32: THE ROOSTER CROWS

Then Jesus' disciples run away, for they are afraid.

Except Peter, who follows Jesus as he is taken to trial, to observe what happens. Two servant girls and some passers-by accuse him in the streets of following Jesus. Three times, Peter denies knowing Jesus, the last time swearing with an oath, "I do not know the man!"

Then the rooster crows. From a distance, Jesus looks back at Peter, who is weeping bitterly.

Matthew 26, Mark 14, Luke 22, John 18

On Trial

LENT DAY 33 (FIFTH SUNDAY OF LENT): ECCE HOMO!

Jesus is placed on trial five times, accused of inciting a riot, advising people to not pay their taxes to the Empire, and blaspheming against both the Jewish religion and the emperor-cult of Rome. Jesus' accusers break the law and tradition to ensure Jesus will be executed.

Pontius Pilate invokes the custom of releasing a prisoner before the Passover, and presents the mob with a choice: release a violent man, or release the one who came to teach peace? Thirsty for blood, the crowd demands Jesus' execution.

Pilate washes his hands, announcing, "I am innocent of this man's blood!" Then he orders Jesus to be executed.

Matthew 27, Mark 14, Luke 23, John 18†

King of the Jews!

LENT DAY 34: A GAME OF STONES AND KNUCKLEBONES

The Roman soldiers loved to play a game called Kings, in which a prisoner was selected to be dressed as a phony king, and a game board was scratched on the ground where the "king" would be praised, honored, tortured, and often killed. The prisoner's fortune would be decided by pebbles on the board, dice made of sheep knucklebones and small reeds to move the stones.

The game is extended to Jesus. Soldiers spit on him, beat him, place a crown of thorns on his head, and place on him a royal purple robe. The soldiers give him a game reed to hold, as if it were a royal scepter. They bow and sarcastically pay homage, "Hail, King of the Jews!"

Then they take their reeds and strike him, wishing they could have the pleasure of killing Jesus themselves.

Matthew 27, Mark 15, Luke 22, John 19†

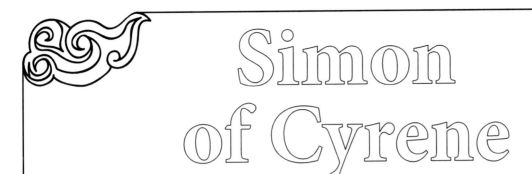

Simon of Cyrene

LENT DAY 35: IS ANY SORROW LIKE MY SORROW?

Under the gaze of his mother, Jesus—thirsty, hungry, bleeding, tired, and facing his own death—falls on the narrow streets of the Holy City while carrying the cross.

An African passer-by, Simon of Cyrene, is compelled by the Roman soldiers to take up the cross and bear it for Jesus to the site of his execution.

Matthew 27, Mark 15, Luke 23

Out of the Crowd

LENT DAY 36: TO THE LEAST OF THESE

"He was despised, marginalized, ostracized, and rejected by them," an anonymous prophet wrote long ago. In horror, "they hid their faces from him!"

But out of the crowd Veronica directly approaches Jesus, who is struggling to walk. She comforts and consoles Jesus, and wipes the blood from his wounds and sweat from his face.

Isaiah 53†

Daughters of Jerusalem

LENT DAY 37: DO NOT WEEP FOR ME

Then the young women and virgins of the city look upon Jesus and cry out in agony, beating their breasts in lament. For it is written in the Song of Songs: "Go out into the streets, daughters of Jerusalem, and look upon the King whose mother, a survivor, crowned him on his wedding day."

Jesus responds, "Do not weep for me, instead weep for yourselves, for the time that is coming will be so cursed that you whose breasts are dry will be blessed for having never bore children!"

Song of Songs 3, Luke 23

LENT DAY 38:
AT GOLGOTHA

Arriving at the place called The Skull, Jesus is nailed to the cross as the crowd mocks him, laughing, spitting, and yelling. The criminals hanging crucified next to Jesus also begin to mock him.

The other condemned criminal shames the others, asking, "Don't you fear God? God is dying here with us, innocently sentenced, and we are guilty!"

He turns his head to Jesus, requesting, "Remember me when you enter your Kingdom."

Jesus answers him, "As we die together, on this day we shall feast in the Kingdom!"

The bored soldiers decide to gamble for Jesus' remaining clothes, a single piece of linen.

Matthew 27, Mark 15, Luke 23, John 19†

The Skull

My God

LENT DAY 39: WHY HAVE YOU ABANDONED ME?

As the Cloud of darkness covers the earth, Jesus cries out in dereliction: "Eli, Eli, lema sabachthani?"

The cityfolk think he is invoking a country-dweller custom to appeal to Elijah as an intercessor, since Elijah did not experience human death, but instead ascended to heaven.

Jesus' words were from the song of King David: "I am not human, but a worm. The mockers call on me to ask for a rescuer. I am poured out like water; dogs and bulls surround me. Why are you so far away; my God, my God, why have You forsaken me?"

Psalm 22, Matthew 27, Mark 15 Luke 23†

Final Command

LENT DAY 40 (PALM AND PASSION SUNDAY):
SHE IS NOW YOUR MOTHER.

In the crowd, Jesus sees his Mother, his aunt Mary, Salome, the disciple whom Jesus loved, and a few others he knew from Galilee.

From the cross Jesus utters to his mother, "Here is your son," and gives a final command to the loved disciple, "This is now your mother."

Matthew 27, Mark 15,
Luke 23, John 19

A Prayer

FOR HOLY WEEK:
PREPARATION TO ENTER A NEW TEMPLE

The Cloud dissipates.

The Holy Temple stands ready to crumble.

The Incarnated is perishing.

A new Temple is being prepared, no longer invoking the Cloud with the blood of goats or the ashes of a heifer.

May we in like manner encourage each other in our shared task of preparing our hearts to be liberated sepulchres of the Divine, which pours out perpetually as love for one another and especially for the poor and the hopeless.

Amen.

Hebrews 9, 10†

Into Your Hands

LENT DAY 41: HOLY AND GREAT MONDAY

Dying of doubt more than asphyxiation, Jesus prays again, "Into your hands I commend my spirit," adding, "it is finished," and takes his final breath.

Matthew 27, Mark 15, Luke 23, John 19†

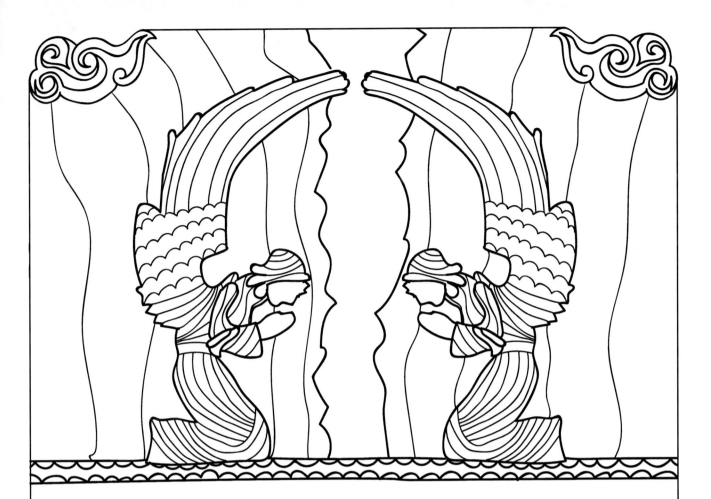

The Death of God

LENT DAY 42: HOLY AND GREAT TUESDAY

In the days of the High Priest Eli, when the Ark of the Covenant was captured at the Battle of Eben-Ezer, the Philistines brought it into the Temple in Ashdod and placed it before the idol of Dagon. Over two nights, before the Ark the statue of Dagon fell twice; the second time it was decapitated and dismembered.

When Eli's daughter-in-law heard of Eli's death in the battle and the capture of the Ark of the Covenant, she prematurely gave birth to a boy, named Ichabod, which means "glory has departed Israel."

In like manner, at the moment of Jesus' death, the thick curtain in the Holiest Place of the Temple is torn from top to bottom, exposing a vacant space.

The Cloud will no longer there intermingle with the smoke and incense invoked by the fire made by human hands and the sprinkling of blood, or out of a need or desire for animal sacrifices, sacred violence, or ritualized atonement.

1 Samuel 4-5, Matthew 27, Mark 15, Luke 23

The Resurrection of Bodies

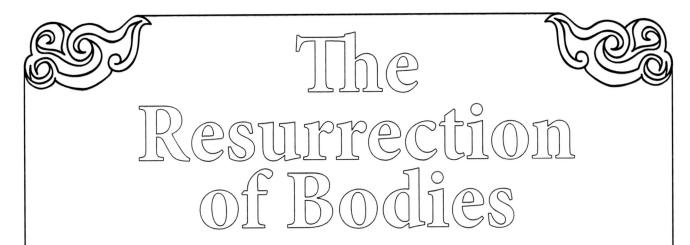

LENT DAY 43: HOLY AND GREAT WEDNESDAY

Suddenly there is an earthquake, which opens the graves of some of the dead, and they awake from the sleep of death. After the resurrection of Jesus, they walk out of their graves and enter the city.

Matthew 27

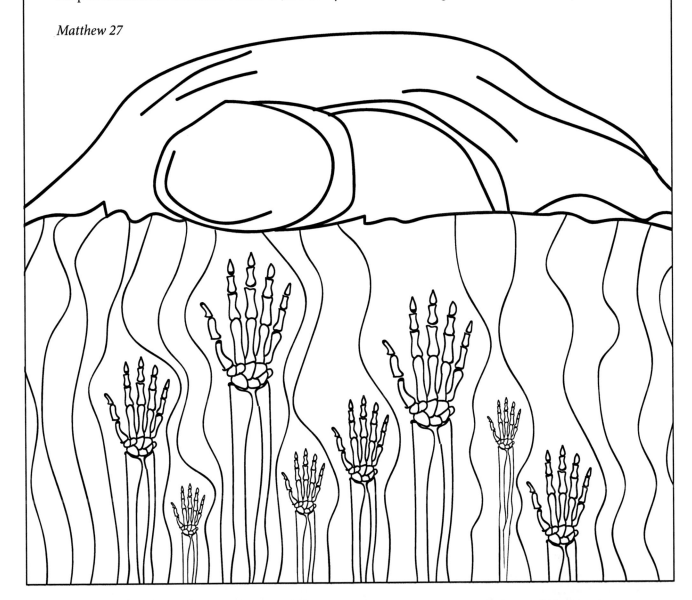

The Burial of God

LENT DAY 44: MAUNDY THURSDAY

Because of the religious festivities and observances, the bodies of the crucified needed to be removed immediately if they were to receive proper burial. A wealthy man from Arimathea and dissenting councilman, Joseph, asks Pilate for permission to take Jesus' body.

Nicodemus, who had been taught by Jesus, also comes with myrrh and aloe. He and Joseph wrap Jesus' body in a linen cloth, and bring Jesus to Joseph's own tomb.

Jesus' mother and the other women follow them to the garden tomb just outside the city walls, and watch as Jesus is laid into Joseph's tomb. They return to their homes to prepare more spices for Jesus' body on the following day.

Matthew 27, Mark 15, Luke 23, John 19

The Sealing

LENT DAY 45: GOOD FRIDAY

Concerned that Jesus' followers will claim that Jesus is really alive, Pilate orders that soldiers go to Joseph's tomb, authenticate the body of Jesus, seal the tomb with clay, and place the seal of Imperial Rome upon the clay—indicating the severity of the crime of interfering with the tomb.

The soldiers then keep watch, guarding the tomb all night.

Matthew 27

The Harrowing

LENT DAY 46: HOLY SATURDAY

The Cloud dissipates and vanishes from the earth! Jesus descends into hell, and there proclaims the Good News to the dead, many of whom have been asleep.

John the Baptist had prepared the way for the children of Adam in hell, and the love of Jesus covered the multitude of the damned. Many of them had been killed in the Great Flood or covered by the Red Sea; but now the waters of baptism save them, and us, through the miracle of the Cloud's next adventure into human flesh.

1 Peter 3

A Prayer

FOR THE EASTER VIGIL

O God, I am counted among those who dwell in hell, for I have forsaken the inexhaustible fountain of Your Word. Guide us now to be strong, to have understanding, that wherever there is a length to the days, or wherever there is life, we might find Holy Wisdom with Your Light and Your Peace.

May we be turned toward Her, for She has lived among us and has commanded the leopards of the mountains; She is the Law and Commandments of the people of old. May we be drawn to Her Light, and may that Light live in our hearts and be spoken on our lips.

Living within us, we have intermixed the bread and wine, which She has offered to us, so our footsteps may be guided by Her Light, our tongues be the language of justice and righteousness, and Her Wisdom perfume every tomb and ambry we liberate, and bestow upon the humble the fullness of Her treasures of Love.

Amen.

Proverbs 8, Song of Songs 4, Baruch 3

Death Transfigures

EASTER SUNRISE

Now, out of the darkness, God, arise into the Light!

Rise up, so we might become enfleshed with your Light and become children of the Light.

In the Light, the bare nakedness of the world is exposed,

Having been nailed to the cross,

Calling upon those who slumber:

The Anointing of Christ will arrive!

Amen!

Ephesians 5

Flesh Transfigures

EASTER MORNING

The women come to the tomb with anointing spices early the next morning to discover that the tomb has been opened. Terrified, Mary Magdalene tells Peter and the disciple Jesus loved what has happened, and they run to the tomb to find it empty except for a linen cloth.

While the disciples return home amazed and perplexed, Mary Magdalene sits behind and weeps.

Then she sees two angels inside of the tomb, dazzling white, like lightning!

And they speak! "Do not be afraid! Why do you weep? Why are you searching for the living among the dead?"

A voice from behind her asks her the same question: "Why do you weep?" and then calls her by name.

She then recognizes Jesus. "Rabbouni!" They embrace.

"Do not hold on to my body," he says, "for I have not yet ascended. But tell the others, and I will meet them in Galilee. Do not be afraid!"

The woman runs away in terror and excitement to tell the others who do not believe, are hiding, or have abandoned Jesus.

Matthew 28, Mark 16, Luke 24, John 20

Why Are You Afraid?

EASTER EVENING

The disciples and followers of Jesus gather in Jerusalem. Some of them believe that they have seen Jesus alive; some recognize him in the taking, blessing, and breaking of bread.

Among the small crowd, a voice announces, "Peace be with you!" Then Jesus reveals himself to them.

Believing Jesus to be a ghost, they are astonished and terrified. He asks, "Why are you afraid? Why do you doubt? Touch my flesh; ghosts do not have flesh such as this."

As they stand in wonderment, he adds, "I'm hungry, do you have something to eat?"

Jesus then teaches them: "You are witnesses to the unfolding, enfolding, and encircling of scripture, which began with God speaking creation. And as I now speak, and you will speak, we are now living scripture and establishing the New Creation!"

Luke 24

Anamnesis

POSTSCRIPT

We have received these instructions from the Cloud, made flesh, who has dwelled among us. When we share bread and wine with those who are faithful and those who doubt, and express genuine thankfulness, we remember the dismemberment of the Cloud into the history of the faithful, and then into the flesh of all who share this world into which the Christ was incarnated.

For when we remember the dismembered, we proclaim the death of God as we wait faithfully for the completion of the Age of Pentecost and God arrives again through the Cloud.

Amen.

1 Corinthians 11†

Benediction

Now go, and break the seal of the entombments around you and others. Like Jesus, smash open the gates of hell in those places where there is only death, bringing new life!

You have been given this new life through the Cloud, which speaks through Fire, Water, and Mist: you are anointed with Christ newly as Priest of the Order of Melchizedek, Prophet in the tradition of the Isaiahs, and King from the cursed lineage of David.

With your authority may you preach to all that you meet the Good News of the chrism of salvation, and building the Kingdom of God, and the reversal of the world in the name of the Alpha and Omega, as a member of the living Body of Christ which arrives through and with the Cloud.

For on this day, and every day that follows, shall the scriptures be fulfilled in your hearing.

Amen.

Psalm 89, Isaiah 61, Luke 4, Revelation 1†

Epigraph

Clean Monday is the Monday before Ash Wednesday in the Orthodox tradition. It is a day of purification and flying colorful kites.

St. Ephrem the Syrian (c. 306-373) was a fourth-century Syriac Christian deacon and theologian best known for his hymns.

Day 1: Ash Wednesday

Absolute exhaustion: God exhausts Godself into Christ as an act of kenosis, or self-negation (Philippians 2). Here we make reference to the radical theology of Thomas Altizer, whose work inspires us. The primary idea of his enormously difficult theology is that kenosis is the history of creation, as well as the history of sacred scripture, exhausting into the incarnation of Jesus. Altizer's key works relevant to this work are *Radical Theology and the Death of God* (with William Hamilton, 1968), *The Descent into Hell* (1970), *The Self-Embodiment of God* (1977), *Total Presence* (1980), *The New Gospel of Christian Atheism* (2002), *Living the Death of God* (2006), and *The Apocalyptic Trinity* (2012).

The image of the cloud is an important and pervasive symbol of theophany and apocalypse in the Bible, particularly in the Hebrew scriptures. Even though the symbol never went away, it has been newly mined in the stunning theopoetic work of Catherine Keller, *Cloud of the Impossible* (New York: Columbia Univ. Press, 2014).

In this work we employ the cloud because of its literal connections to several of these stories, but also to reclaim the image for our shared reality of the post-Christendom church after the death of God. Perhaps stated in a banal way, "How do you include 'God' in a coloring book?" Practically speaking, the "Cloud" allows us to avoid gendered or pedestrian imagery for the divine. But beyond this the cloud may be colorless, take many colors, take shapes real or imagined, and may reflect increasing cloudiness or dissipating clouds—and all of the rich and robust theological implications for these ideas.

The little bird…strikes the walls of its cage: from Friedrich Nietzsche, *The Gay Science*, trans. W. Kaufmann (New York: Vintage, 1974), §123 ("In the Horizon of the Infinite," immediately before the infamous aphorism, "The Madman").

Day 3: Children of Adam

This scripture's connection to the larger narrative within this work is grounded in the thought of Rene Girard—see, for example, Girard, *Things Hidden Since the Foundation of the World*, trans. S. Bann and M. Metteer (Stanford, CA: Stanford Univ. Press, 1987), 142ff. Girard's mimetic theory of violence is a key theme of this present work as a radical interpretation of Christian scripture.

Day 5: Job Meditates on Death and New Life

Note that while there are forty "days" of Lent, the Sundays of Lent are not counted among the forty days. For simplicity, we include the Sundays as days on the Lenten coloring journey.

Day 11: Snakes on a Plain

The Nehushtan or Nohestan is later destroyed by order of King Hezekiah (2 Kings 18) to purge latent paganism from the Israelite religious practices. In John 3 Jesus likens the rising of the Son of Man to the symbolism of healing of the Nehushtan.

Day 13: Qui Habitat

Qui Habitat is the well-known Latin title for Psalm 91, after the first words of the Psalm ("whoso dweleth"), and is also known as the "Psalm of Protection."

The authorship of Psalm 91 is disputed to be either Moses or David.

Day 17: The Cloud Will Be Enfleshed

This prophesy is from Deutero-Isaiah, from the second part of the Book of Isaiah. Scholars believe that Isaiah was initially written by Isaiah ben Amoz, and his ideas were continued and expanded anonymously in what would become the second and third "parts" of the Book of Isaiah.

Day 19: Not to Be Tested

The pinnacle of the Second Temple would have looked down into the Kidron Valley to where the tombs of Absalom and Zechariah stand today. It is unlikely that the tomb of Absalom was there during Jesus' time. I discuss this topography in Christopher Rodkey, *The World is Crucifixion* (Aurora, CO: Noesis, 2016), 55-62.

Day 21: Come out!

Jesus thus steals the corpse: like a "resurrectionist," Jesus interrupts the social order associated with prescribed and professional grieving. For more on this interpretation, see Christopher Rodkey, *The World is Crucifixion*, 73-80.

Day 22: In Bethany

For more on the significance of the ketoret in the Biblical tradition, see Rodkey, *The World is Crucifixion*, 76-77.

Day 23: The Parade of Palms

For more on this interpretation of the Procession of Palms, see Christopher Rodkey, *Too Good to Be True* (Winchester, UK: Christian Alternative, 2014), 108-14.

Day 33: Ecce Homo!

Ecce Homo is Latin for "Here is" or "Behold the Man!" According to the Latin Vulgate translation of John 19, Pilate uses these words to present Jesus to the mob. The phrase is also the title of Nietzsche's final work, in which he places himself on trial; the work is subtitled Wie man wird, was man ist, that is, How One Becomes What One Is.

Given Jesus' question of identity, "Who do you say that I am?" (Mark 8:29, Matthew 16:15) we make the connection here that Jesus is becoming what even Pilate says in his presentation to the angry crowd. Through the trial, Jesus is becoming the archetype for humanity.

Day 34: A Game of Stones and Knucklebones
The carvings for this game, Basileus, can be seen anywhere one would have found Roman soldiers, and can be plainly seen in Israel today.

Day 36: To the Least of These
This apocryphal—that is, not found in the Bible—story is one with deep roots in ancient church tradition. This tradition teaches that a woman named St. Veronica (from vera icon, or "true image"), watching Jesus walking through the narrow streets of Jerusalem, gave Jesus her veil to wipe the blood from his face. Centuries later several relics emerged claiming to be this veil, bearing the image of Christ on Veronica's veil. We include this story here not only because of its important history but because St. Veronica remains important to many Christian traditions and is an essential element of the Via Dolorosa.

Day 38: At Golgotha
The image here makes a connection to the theme of the Nehushtan in our narrative, with the serpent, but also a nod to the artistic tradition of a skull at the foot of the cross. The symbolism is that the site of Jesus' crucifixion is also the long-lost site of the grave of Adam; another tradition holds that the place is called "The Skull" because a nearby rock formation that appears to be a skull is the remnants of the head of Goliath, placed on this site by David.

Day 39: Why Have You Abandoned Me?
"Eli, Eli, lema sabachthani?" is Aramaic for "My God, my God, why have you abandoned me?" In the radical theology tradition (in particular, Altizer and Slavoj Žižek), this is interpreted to imply that any hope for the interventionist, "Big Other" God is about to die with Jesus' cry of abandonment from the cross. For a deeper explanation of this, see Marcus Pound, *Žižek: A (Very) Critical Introduction* (Grand Rapids, MI: Eerdmans, 2008), 23-52 and Adam Kotsko, *Žižek and Theology* (New York: T & T Clark, 2008), 94-95.

A Prayer for Holy Week
The language here is intentionally meant to reference Nietzsche's parable of the madman—"the sepulchers of God," "what sacred games shall we have to invent?"— in *The Gay Science,* §125. The terminology of a perishing deity is again a reference to the radical theology of Altizer.

The days following this prayer are the days of Holy Week. Note that the lectionary readings for these days do not squarely align with the pages for these pages; please consult the lectionary index to locate these texts.

Day 41: Holy and Great Monday

If Jesus' Aramaic words of dereliction indicate an end to the belief in a "Big Other" God (see notes above for Day 39), these words here take new meaning.

Postscript: Anamnesis

Anamnesis means "remembering" and is closely associated with Plato's epistemology. In the Christian tradition, anamnesis refers to the act of memorializing Christ in the Eucharist (and used by Jesus--"ἀνάμνησιν"--in Luke 22:19) and the liturgical act of remembering God's actions related to salvation history.

The Benediction: Chrism Mass

The Chrism Mass is a special liturgical observation performed on Maundy Thursday by Roman Catholic Bishops, usually with the local priests in attendance, to bless the three kinds of anointing oils ("chrism") that will be used by the priests to administer sacraments in the coming year.

SCRIPTURE REFERENCES

SCRIPTURAL INDEX

LECTIONARY INDEX